Juices are a delicious and healthy option that offers a convenient way to consume a wide variety of essential nutrients in a single drink. By mixing fruits, vegetables, seeds, and other nutritious ingredients, we can create juices that are true health concentrates, providing unparalleled benefits for our body.

1

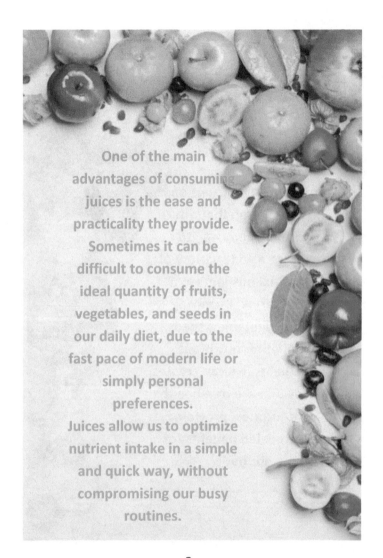

One of the main advantages of consuming juices is the ease and practicality they provide. Sometimes it can be difficult to consume the ideal quantity of fruits, vegetables, and seeds in our daily diet, due to the fast pace of modern life or simply personal preferences.

Juices allow us to optimize nutrient intake in a simple and quick way, without compromising our busy routines.

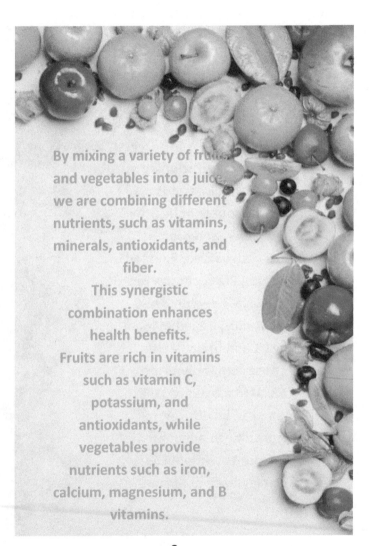

By mixing a variety of fruits and vegetables into a juice, we are combining different nutrients, such as vitamins, minerals, antioxidants, and fiber.
This synergistic combination enhances health benefits.
Fruits are rich in vitamins such as vitamin C, potassium, and antioxidants, while vegetables provide nutrients such as iron, calcium, magnesium, and B vitamins.

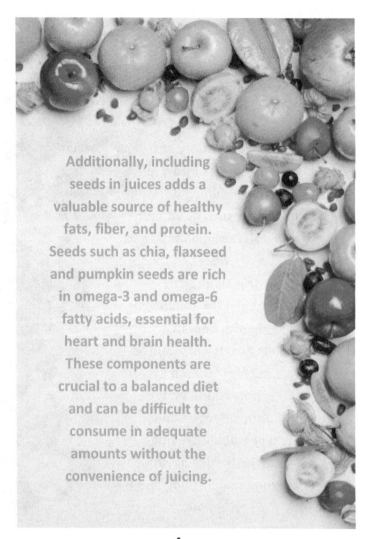

Additionally, including seeds in juices adds a valuable source of healthy fats, fiber, and protein. Seeds such as chia, flaxseed and pumpkin seeds are rich in omega-3 and omega-6 fatty acids, essential for heart and brain health. These components are crucial to a balanced diet and can be difficult to consume in adequate amounts without the convenience of juicing.

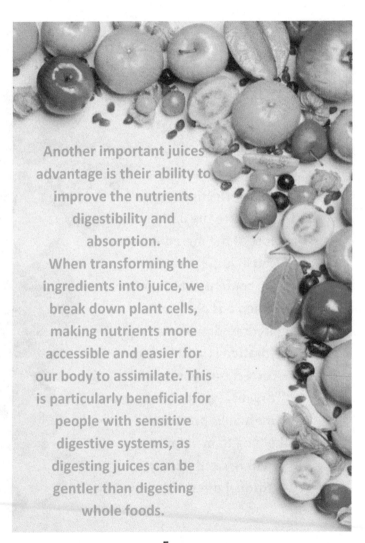

Another important juices advantage is their ability to improve the nutrients digestibility and absorption.
When transforming the ingredients into juice, we break down plant cells, making nutrients more accessible and easier for our body to assimilate. This is particularly beneficial for people with sensitive digestive systems, as digesting juices can be gentler than digesting whole foods.

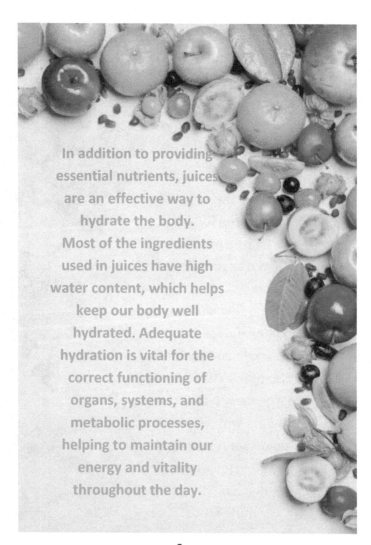

In addition to providing
essential nutrients, juices
are an effective way to
hydrate the body.
Most of the ingredients
used in juices have high
water content, which helps
keep our body well
hydrated. Adequate
hydration is vital for the
correct functioning of
organs, systems, and
metabolic processes,
helping to maintain our
energy and vitality
throughout the day.

Natural juices, by combining a variety of nutrient-rich ingredients, become powerful allies in the quest to eliminate body weight in a healthy way.

These drinks, loaded with vitamins, minerals, antioxidants and fiber, have the potential to boost health and help achieve a more balanced and fit body.

One of the primary benefits of juices for those looking to reduce weight is their ability to promote satiety. By including ingredients rich in fiber, such as fruits, vegetables and seeds, juices provide a feeling of fullness that helps control appetite and prevent overeating. This is essential to maintain an adequate calorie balance and, consequently, contribute to weight loss and size reduction.

The presence of essential nutrients such as vitamins and minerals in juices is also crucial for the body's healthy metabolism. These substances help in the efficient functioning of the metabolic system, which can result in greater calorie burning and the optimization of digestion and nutrient absorption processes. In this way, the juices help to promote an active metabolism, contributing to fat loss and muscle toning.

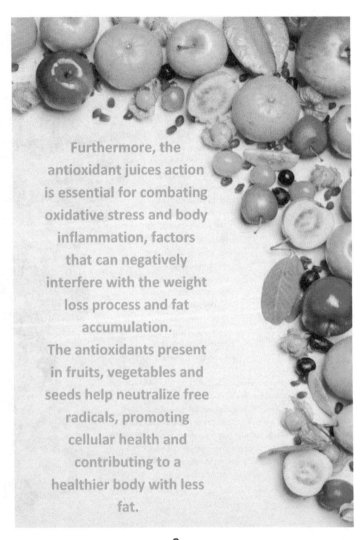

Furthermore, the antioxidant juices action is essential for combating oxidative stress and body inflammation, factors that can negatively interfere with the weight loss process and fat accumulation.
The antioxidants present in fruits, vegetables and seeds help neutralize free radicals, promoting cellular health and contributing to a healthier body with less fat.

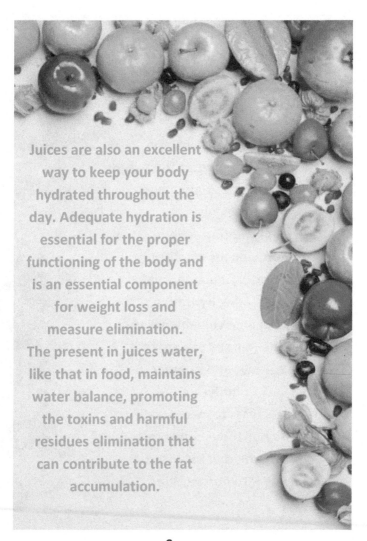

Juices are also an excellent way to keep your body hydrated throughout the day. Adequate hydration is essential for the proper functioning of the body and is an essential component for weight loss and measure elimination. The present in juices water, like that in food, maintains water balance, promoting the toxins and harmful residues elimination that can contribute to the fat accumulation.

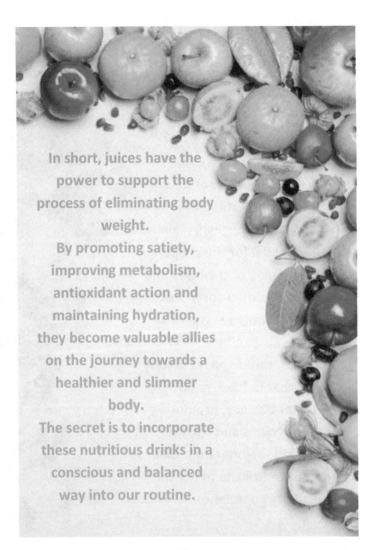

In short, juices have the
power to support the
process of eliminating body
weight.
By promoting satiety,
improving metabolism,
antioxidant action and
maintaining hydration,
they become valuable allies
on the journey towards a
healthier and slimmer
body.
The secret is to incorporate
these nutritious drinks in a
conscious and balanced
way into our routine.

MAIN FRUITS

WE

WILL USE.

Acerola - Iron, vitamin A, vitamin B5, vitamin C.

Pineapple - Manganese, vitamin A, vitamin B6, vitamin C.

Plum – Fiber, potassium, vitamin C, vitamin K.

Blackberry – Fiber, potassium, vitamin C, vitamin K.

Banana – Fiber, potassium, vitamin B6, vitamin C.

Cashew - Iron, magnesium, vitamin C, vitamin K.

Persimmon - Fiber, potassium, vitamin A, vitamin C.

Carrot – Potassium, vitamin A, vitamin B6, vitamin K.

Cherry - Antioxidants, potassium, vitamin A, vitamin C.

Fig - Calcium, potassium, vitamin A, vitamin K.

Raspberry – Fiber, manganese, vitamin C, vitamin K.

Guava - Fiber, vitamin A, vitamin C, vitamin E.

Kiwi - Potassium, vitamin C, vitamin E, vitamin K.

Orange – Folate, potassium, vitamin A, vitamin C.

Lychee - Potassium, vitamin B6, vitamin C, vitamin E.

Lemon – Citric acid, potassium, vitamin C.

Papaya - Folate, vitamin A, vitamin C, vitamin E.

Mango - Folate, vitamin A, vitamin C, vitamin E.

Watermelon - Lycopene, potassium, vitamin A, vitamin C.

Melon – Folate, potassium, vitamin A, vitamin C.

Blueberry – Antioxidants, fiber, vitamin C, vitamin K.

Strawberry – Folate, potassium, vitamin C, vitamin K.

Pear – Fiber, potassium, vitamin C, vitamin K.

Peach – Potassium, vitamin A, vitamin C, vitamin K.

Tangerine - Folate, potassium, vitamin A, vitamin C.

Grape - Potassium, resveratrol, vitamin C, vitamin K.

Beet -
Vitamin A, Vitamin C, Fiber,
Iron, Potassium, Folate.

Cabbage -
Vitamin K, Vitamin A,
Vitamin C, Folate, Iron,
Calcium, Fiber.

Carrot -
Vitamin A, Vitamin C,
Vitamin K, Potassium, Fiber.

Spinach -
Vitamin A, Vitamin C,
Vitamin K, Iron, Acid folic
Acid, Magnesium.

HONEY

Sugars: The main component of honey is sugar, mainly glucose and fructose.

Water: Honey contains a significant amount of water.

Carbohydrates: In addition to sugars, honey has a small amount of other carbohydrates such as oligosaccharides.

Vitamins: Honey contains small amounts of several vitamins, including vitamin C, niacin, riboflavin, pantothenic acid, vitamin B6 and folate.

Minerals: Honey contains essential minerals, including calcium, iron, magnesium, phosphorus, potassium, sodium, zinc, and selenium.

Antioxidants: Honey contains antioxidant compounds, such as flavonoids and phenols, which can help neutralize free radicals in the body.

Enzymes: Honey contains natural enzymes, such as glucose oxidase, which can help break down glucose and produce hydrogen peroxide, an antimicrobial agent.

Amino acids: Honey contains a small quantity of amino acids, the building blocks of proteins.

Organic Acids: Honey contains several organic acids, including acetic acid, citric acid, lactic acid, and malic acid.

Antimicrobial substances: Honey has antimicrobial properties due to the presence of compounds such as hydrogen peroxide, low pH, and other components.

Flavonoids: Honey contains flavonoids, which are antioxidant compounds that may have health benefits.

SEEDS

Nut: Found in various parts of the world, rich in omega-3 fatty acids, proteins, fiber, vitamins, and minerals.

Brazil nut (originally from the Amazon) is an excellent source of selenium, in addition to providing healthy fats, proteins and fiber.

Almond: Originally from the Middle East, rich in vitamin E, fiber, proteins, healthy fats, calcium, magnesium, and iron.

Hazelnut: Common in Europe and Asia, it is a good source of vitamin E, folic acid, healthy fats, and proteins.

Cashew nuts: Originally from Brazil, they are a good source of copper, magnesium, phosphorus, proteins, and healthy fats.

Macadamia: Originally from Australia, is rich in monounsaturated fats, thiamine, manganese, and magnesium.

Pistachio: Originally from Western Asia, is a good source of protein, fiber, potassium, vitamin B6 and antioxidants.

TURMERIC

Curcumin: Curcumin is the main active component of turmeric and is a powerful antioxidant and anti-inflammatory. It's responsible for the characteristic yellow color of turmeric.

Curcuminoids: In addition to curcumin, turmeric contains other curcuminoids that also have antioxidant and anti-inflammatory properties.

Vitamins and Minerals: Turmeric contains a variety of vitamins and minerals, including vitamin C, vitamin E, vitamin K, iron, potassium, and calcium.

Essential Oils: Turmeric contains essential oils, including turmerone, atlantone and zingiberene, which also contribute to its health benefits.

Key health benefits associated with turmeric include:

Anti-inflammatory Properties: Curcumin has anti-inflammatory properties that can help reducing inflammation in the body.

Antioxidant: Curcumin is an effective antioxidant, combating damage caused by free radicals and helping to protect cells.

Improved Digestive Health: Turmeric can help alleviate digestive disorders, promoting healthy digestion and relieving gastric discomfort.

Possible Benefit against Cancer: Some studies suggest that curcumin may have properties that help prevent or treat certain types of cancer.

Support Heart Health: Turmeric may support heart health by helping regulate blood pressure, reduce cholesterol and improve cardiovascular function.

Support Brain Function: Research indicates that curcumin may have protective effects on the brain and may be beneficial in preventing neurodegenerative diseases such as Alzheimer's.

It is important to note that turmeric is more effective when consumed together with black pepper, as the piperine present in pepper increases the absorption of curcumin in the body.

17

GINGER

In addition to its culinary uses, ginger has been recognized for its health benefits. It contains a variety of essential nutrients that contribute to the body and mind well-being.

Potassium: Ginger is a source of potassium, an important mineral for electrolyte balance in the body. Potassium plays a vital role in the proper functioning of muscles, heart and nervous system.

Magnesium: Magnesium is another mineral found in ginger. It's essential for the bones, muscles and nerves health, in addition to being involved in more than 300 biochemical reactions in the body.

Vitamin B6 (Pyridoxine): Ginger is a source of vitamin B6, which plays a crucial role in brain function, mood regulation and immune system health.

Vitamin C (Ascorbic Acid): Although the amount of vitamin C in ginger is not as high as in some citrus fruits, it still contains a significant amount of this antioxidant vitamin. Vitamin C is vital for the immune system, healthy skin and wound healing.

In addition to these essential nutrients, ginger is known for its anti-inflammatory and antioxidant properties. It contains bioactive compounds such as gingerol, shogaol and zingerone, which have been linked to a variety of health benefits.

Anti-inflammatory Properties: Gingerol, one of the main bioactive compounds in ginger, has anti-inflammatory properties that can help alleviate inflammation in the body. This is particularly beneficial for people with inflammatory diseases such as arthritis.

Nausea Relief: Ginger has a long history of use for relieving nausea and vomiting, especially in pregnant women or people who have undergone medical procedures such as chemotherapy.

Aid Digestion: Ginger can help improve digestion, relieving symptoms of indigestion, abdominal discomfort and nausea associated with digestive disorders.

Weight Loss Potential: Some studies suggest that ginger may increase thermogenesis, which may be beneficial for those trying to lose weight. This means that ginger can help increase your metabolism and burn more calories.

Improves Blood Circulation: Ginger can help improve blood circulation, which is beneficial for cardiovascular health and may reduce the risk of heart disease.

CINNAMON

Cinnamon is a spice originating from Sri Lanka, India and Bangladesh, obtained from the inner bark of the Cinnamomum tree. It's widely used in cooking, both to add flavor and for health benefits. Cinnamon has a sweet, warm flavor, which makes it popular in a variety of sweet and savory dishes. Furthermore, it has several beneficial components, including:

Coumarin: Coumarin is a compound found naturally in cinnamon that can have anticoagulant and anti-inflammatory effects, but in high doses it can be toxic to the liver.

Essential Oils: Cinnamon contains essential oils, such as cinnamaldehyde, eugenol and linalool, which contribute to its characteristic aroma and flavor.

Antioxidants: Cinnamon is rich in antioxidants, which help fight free radicals and protect the body's cells against damage.

Some of the top health benefits associated with cinnamon include:

Blood Sugar Regulation: Cinnamon can help improve insulin sensitivity and reduce blood sugar levels, making it especially useful for people with diabetes or insulin resistance.

Anti-inflammatory Properties: The compounds in cinnamon have anti-inflammatory properties, which can help reduce inflammation in the body and alleviate inflammatory conditions.

Antimicrobial Action: Cinnamon has antimicrobial properties that can help fight infections and reduce the growth of bacteria, fungi and viruses.

Improves Digestive Health: Cinnamon can aid digestion, relieving gastric discomfort, gas and indigestion.

Support Heart Health: Cinnamon may contribute to cardiovascular health by helping to reduce cholesterol and triglyceride levels.

Anticancer Potential: Some studies indicate that cinnamon compounds may have properties that help prevent the growth of cancer cells.

DIETARY GELATIN

Gelatin is made from collagen, a protein found in the connective tissues of animals, such as skin, bones, and cartilage. Gelatin is dissolved in hot water and, when it cools, forms a characteristic gelatinous texture.

Here are some key points about dietary gelatin:

Sweeteners: Diet gelatin uses low- or low-calorie sweeteners to replace sugar, making it a suitable choice for people looking to reduce their sugar intake.

Low Calories: Because it is made with low- or no-calorie sweeteners, diet gelatin generally has fewer calories compared to traditional gelatin.

Protein: Gelatin is a source of protein, although it's an incomplete protein, as it doesn't contain all the essential amino acids needed by the body.

Versatility: Dietary gelatin can be used in a variety of recipes, including desserts, salads, molds, and other dishes.

Flavor Options: Just like traditional gelatin, dietary gelatin is available in a variety of flavors to suit individual preferences.

Special Dietary Requirements: Dietary gelatin can be an option for people who follow diets with carbohydrate restrictions or who are looking for sugar-free options.

The 30-day diet based on the daily consumption of natural juices and the total elimination of sugar and fried foods represents a firm commitment to health and well-being.

This eating regimen aims to promote a balanced and healthy approach to improving nutrition, eliminating empty calories, and establishing a healthier routine.

During this period, each day begins with the preparation and consumption of a fresh, nutritious juice made from a variety of fruits, vegetables, seeds, and other healthy ingredients. These juices are rich in vitamins, minerals, antioxidants, and fiber, providing the body with the nutrients it needs to maintain energy and promote health.

Excluding sugar from your diet is a crucial step toward improving metabolic health and reducing empty calorie intake.
Added sugar, found in many processed products, can lead to weight gain, increased blood sugar levels and other health complications. By avoiding sugary foods and drinks, the diet focuses on natural and whole foods, promoting more balanced nutrition.

Furthermore, the decision to eliminate fried foods and opt for healthier preparation methods, such as baking, is an important step towards reducing the intake of harmful fats and unnecessary calories. Fried foods generally involve the use of oils that can be harmful to health when consumed in excess. By choosing to bake food, we maintain the flavor and texture, but with less fat and calories.

Throughout these 30 days, the juice diet routine and the elimination of sugar and fried foods encourage a more conscious and healthier lifestyle.

Additionally, it can result in tangible benefits such as weight loss, increased energy, improved skin, and improved digestion.

This nutritional approach helps create healthier, lasting eating habits that can be maintained beyond the 30-day period.

DISCOVER

THE JUICES

POWER

1 Refreshing Pineapple Juice:

Fruit: Pineapple
Vegetable: Spinach
Seed: Chia seeds
Turmeric: A pinch
Cinnamon: A pinch
Ginger: A pinch
Honey: To taste

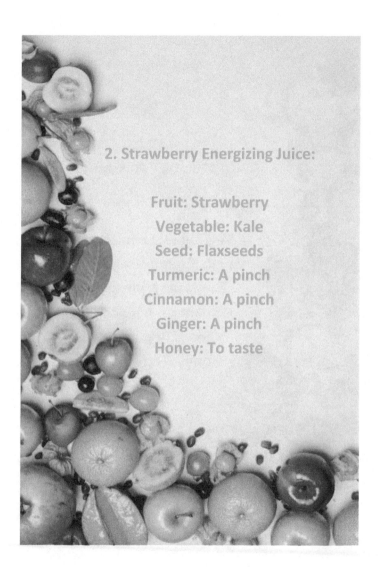

2. Strawberry Energizing Juice:

Fruit: Strawberry
Vegetable: Kale
Seed: Flaxseeds
Turmeric: A pinch
Cinnamon: A pinch
Ginger: A pinch
Honey: To taste

3. Invigorating Apple Juice:

Fruit: Apple
Vegetable: Spinach
Seed: Pumpkin seeds
Turmeric: A pinch
Cinnamon: A pinch
Ginger: A pinch
Honey: To taste

4. Watermelon Detox Juice:

Fruit: Watermelon
Vegetable: Cucumber
Seed: Chia
Turmeric: A pinch
Cinnamon: A pinch
Ginger: A pinch
Honey: To taste

5. Revitalizing Orange Juice:

Fruit: Orange
Vegetable: Spinach
Seed: Sunflower seeds
Turmeric: A pinch
Cinnamon: A pinch
Ginger: A pinch
Honey: To taste

6. Anti-inflammatory Pineapple and Ginger Juice:

Fruit: Pineapple
Vegetable: Celery
Seed: Chia seeds
Turmeric: A pinch
Cinnamon: A pinch
Ginger: A pinch
Honey: To taste

7. Invigorating Juice:

Fruit: Mango
Vegetable: Kale
Seed: Flaxseeds
Turmeric: A pinch
Cinnamon: A pinch
Ginger: A pinch
Honey: To taste

8. Antioxidant Juice:

Fruit: Blueberry
Vegetable: Spinach
Seed: Chia seeds
Turmeric: A pinch
Cinnamon: A pinch
Ginger: A pinch
Honey: To taste

9. Digestive Juice:

Fruit: Pear
Vegetable: Kale
Seed: Pumpkin seeds
Turmeric: A pinch
Cinnamon: A pinch
Ginger: A pinch
Honey: To taste

10. Energizing Juice:

Fruit: Banana
Vegetable: Spinach
Seed: Chia seeds
Turmeric: A pinch
Cinnamon: A pinch
Ginger: A pinch
Honey: To taste

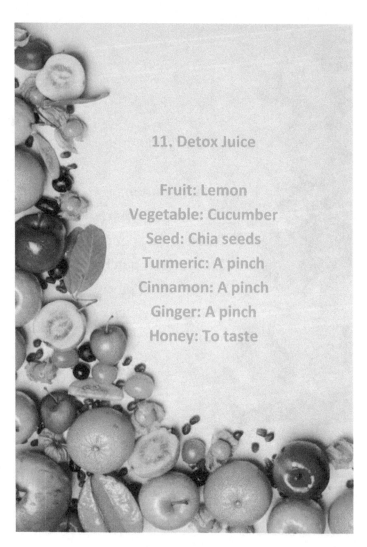

11. Detox Juice

Fruit: Lemon
Vegetable: Cucumber
Seed: Chia seeds
Turmeric: A pinch
Cinnamon: A pinch
Ginger: A pinch
Honey: To taste

12. Revitalizing Juice:

Fruit: Kiwi
Vegetable: Kale
Seed: Linseed
Turmeric: A pinch
Cinnamon: A pinch
Ginger: A pinch
Honey: To taste

13. Beetroot Detox Juice:

Fruit: Beet
Vegetable: Spinach
Seed: Chia
Turmeric: A pinch
Cinnamon: A pinch
Ginger: A pinch
Honey: To taste

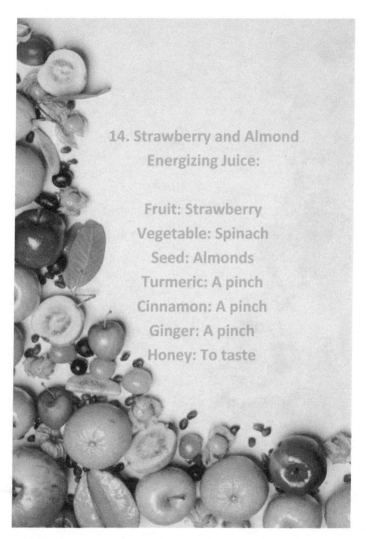

14. Strawberry and Almond Energizing Juice:

Fruit: Strawberry
Vegetable: Spinach
Seed: Almonds
Turmeric: A pinch
Cinnamon: A pinch
Ginger: A pinch
Honey: To taste

15. Refreshing Cucumber Juice:

Fruit: Apple
Green: Cucumber
Seed: Pumpkin seeds
Turmeric: A pinch
Cinnamon: A pinch
Ginger: A pinch
Honey: To taste

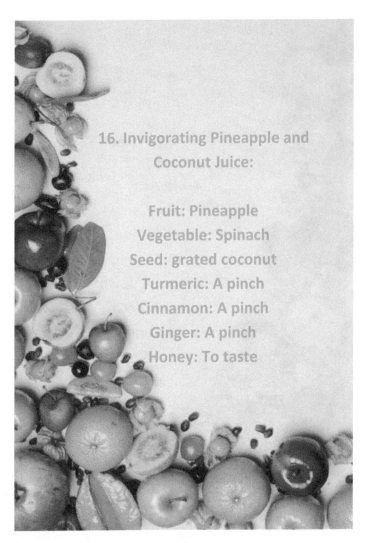

16. Invigorating Pineapple and Coconut Juice:

Fruit: Pineapple
Vegetable: Spinach
Seed: grated coconut
Turmeric: A pinch
Cinnamon: A pinch
Ginger: A pinch
Honey: To taste

17. Acai Antioxidant Juice:

Fruit: Acai
Vegetable: Kale
Seed: Chia seeds
Turmeric: A pinch
Cinnamon: A pinch
Ginger: A pinch
Honey: To taste

18. Revitalizing Pomegranate Juice:

Fruit: Pomegranate
Vegetable: Spinach
Seed: Flaxseeds
Turmeric: A pinch
Cinnamon: A pinch
Ginger: A pinch
Honey: To taste

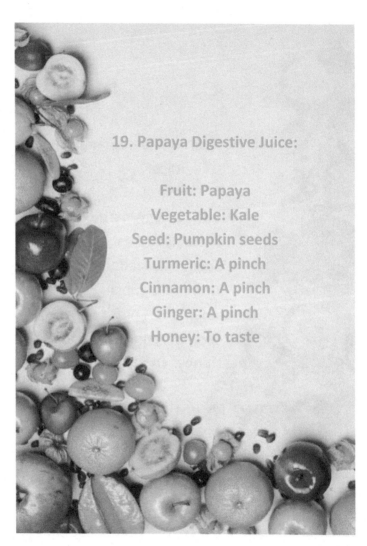

19. Papaya Digestive Juice:

Fruit: Papaya
Vegetable: Kale
Seed: Pumpkin seeds
Turmeric: A pinch
Cinnamon: A pinch
Ginger: A pinch
Honey: To taste

20. Energizing Juice:

Fruit: Grape
Vegetable: Spinach
Seed: Chia seeds
Turmeric: A pinch
Cinnamon: A pinch
Ginger: A pinch
Honey: To taste

21. Revitalizing Juice:

Fruit: Passion fruit
Vegetable: Kale
Seed: Flaxseeds
Turmeric: A pinch
Cinnamon: A pinch
Ginger: A pinch
Honey: To taste

22.Detox Juice :

Fruit: Pineapple
Vegetable: Spinach
Seed: Chia seeds
Turmeric: A pinch
Cinnamon: A pinch
Ginger: A pinch
Honey: To taste

23. Invigorating Ginger Juice:

Fruit: Apple
Vegetable: Spinach
Seed: Pumpkin seeds
Turmeric: A pinch
Cinnamon: A pinch
Ginger: A pinch
Honey: To taste

24. Acerola Antioxidant Juice:

Fruit: Acerola
Vegetable: Kale
Seed: Chia seeds
Turmeric: A pinch
Cinnamon: A pinch
Ginger: A pinch
Honey: To taste

25. Refreshing Lemon and Mint Juice:

Fruit: Lemon
Vegetable: Spinach
Seed: Flaxseeds
Turmeric: A pinch
Cinnamon: A pinch
Ginger: A pinch
Honey: To taste

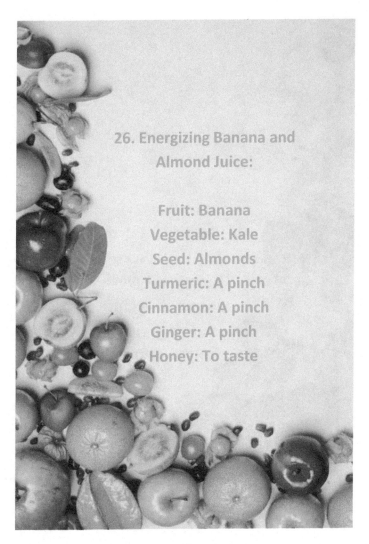

26. Energizing Banana and Almond Juice:

Fruit: Banana
Vegetable: Kale
Seed: Almonds
Turmeric: A pinch
Cinnamon: A pinch
Ginger: A pinch
Honey: To taste

27. Beetroot and Carrot Detox Juice:

Fruit: Beet
Vegetable: Carrot
Seed: Chia seeds
Turmeric: A pinch
Cinnamon: A pinch
Ginger: A pinch
Honey: To taste

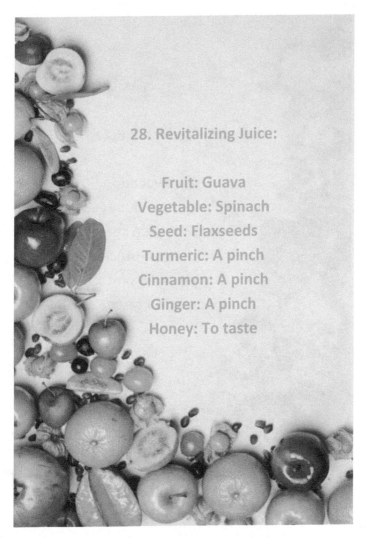

28. Revitalizing Juice:

Fruit: Guava
Vegetable: Spinach
Seed: Flaxseeds
Turmeric: A pinch
Cinnamon: A pinch
Ginger: A pinch
Honey: To taste

29. Digestive Juice:

Fruit: Avocado
Vegetable: Kale
Seed: Pumpkin seeds
Turmeric: A pinch
Cinnamon: A pinch
Honey: To taste

30. Energizing Juice:

Fruit: Peach
Vegetable: Spinach
Seed: Chia seeds
Turmeric: A pinch
Cinnamon: A pinch
Honey: To taste

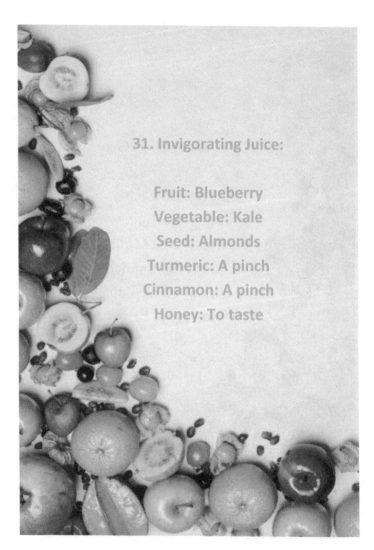

31. Invigorating Juice:

Fruit: Blueberry
Vegetable: Kale
Seed: Almonds
Turmeric: A pinch
Cinnamon: A pinch
Honey: To taste

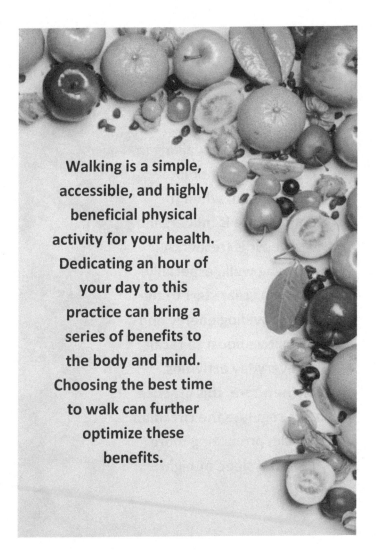

Walking is a simple, accessible, and highly beneficial physical activity for your health. Dedicating an hour of your day to this practice can bring a series of benefits to the body and mind. Choosing the best time to walk can further optimize these benefits.

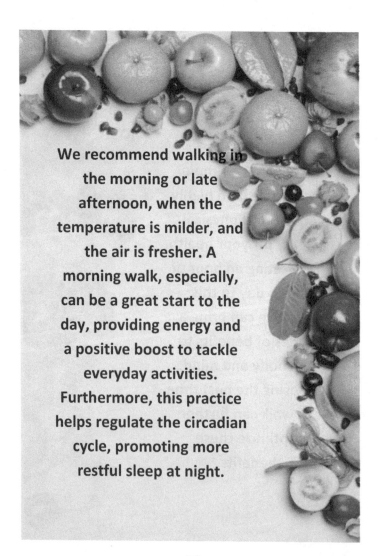

We recommend walking in the morning or late afternoon, when the temperature is milder, and the air is fresher. A morning walk, especially, can be a great start to the day, providing energy and a positive boost to tackle everyday activities. Furthermore, this practice helps regulate the circadian cycle, promoting more restful sleep at night.

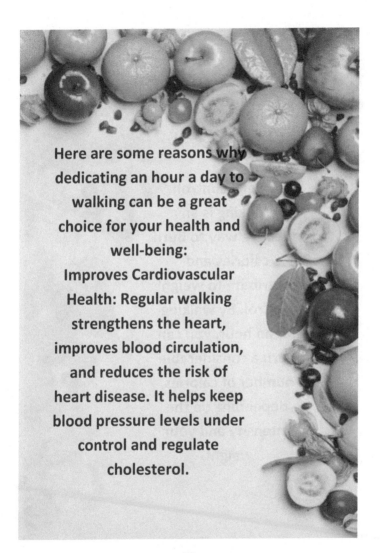

Here are some reasons why dedicating an hour a day to walking can be a great choice for your health and well-being:

Improves Cardiovascular Health: Regular walking strengthens the heart, improves blood circulation, and reduces the risk of heart disease. It helps keep blood pressure levels under control and regulate cholesterol.

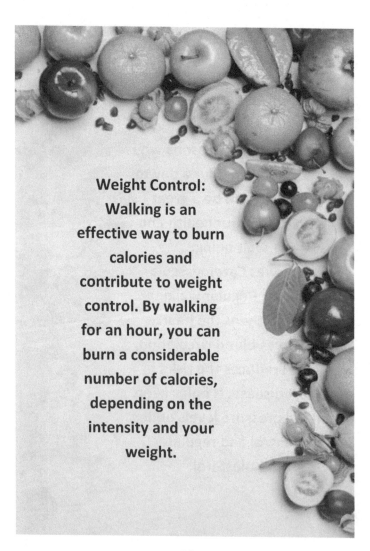

Weight Control:
Walking is an effective way to burn calories and contribute to weight control. By walking for an hour, you can burn a considerable number of calories, depending on the intensity and your weight.

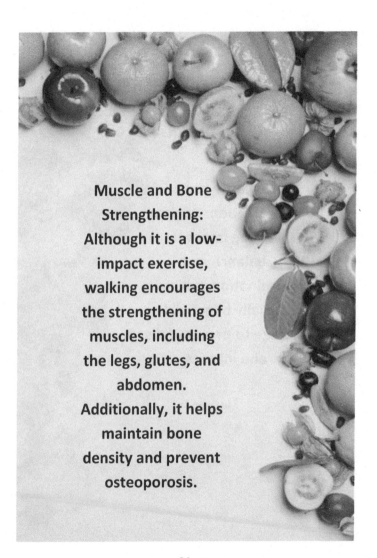

Muscle and Bone Strengthening: Although it is a low-impact exercise, walking encourages the strengthening of muscles, including the legs, glutes, and abdomen. Additionally, it helps maintain bone density and prevent osteoporosis.

Balance and Coordination: Regular walking improves balance and coordination, which is especially beneficial as we age to prevent falls and injuries.

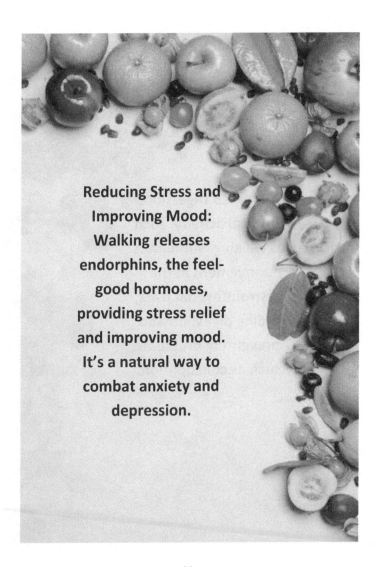

Reducing Stress and Improving Mood: Walking releases endorphins, the feel-good hormones, providing stress relief and improving mood. It's a natural way to combat anxiety and depression.

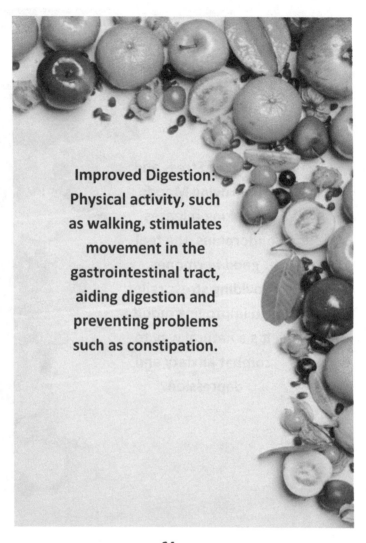

Improved Digestion: Physical activity, such as walking, stimulates movement in the gastrointestinal tract, aiding digestion and preventing problems such as constipation.

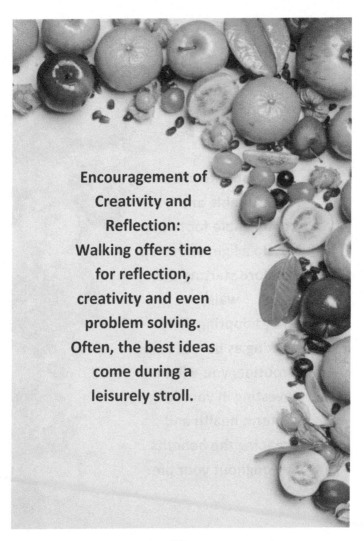

Encouragement of
Creativity and
Reflection:
Walking offers time
for reflection,
creativity and even
problem solving.
Often, the best ideas
come during a
leisurely stroll.

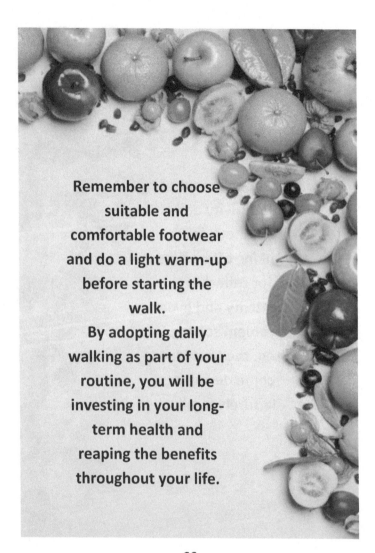

Remember to choose suitable and comfortable footwear and do a light warm-up before starting the walk.

By adopting daily walking as part of your routine, you will be investing in your long-term health and reaping the benefits throughout your life.

Today is the day to embrace positive change! Starting this diet is a courageous step towards the best version of yourself. By prioritizing natural and healthy foods, you are choosing to take care of your body and mind. With each fresh juice, you nourish yourself with essential vitamins and minerals, rejecting harmful sugars and fried foods. This is the path to a healthier body, renewed energy and strengthened self-esteem. Don't wait for tomorrow, start now. The decision is in your hands, and the reward will be a more vibrant life, full of vitality and well-being. You deserve!

108 TIPS

FOR

A

HEALTHY DIET

Exercise regularly and intensely.

Eat more vegetables and fruits.

Reduce your sugar intake.

Drink lots of water daily.

Consume lean proteins daily.

Avoid ultra-processed foods.

Get enough sleep.

Do resistance exercises.

Practice aerobic activities regularly.

Control food portions.

Include fiber in your daily diet.

Eat more frequent and smaller meals.

Avoid fried and fatty foods.

Limit carbohydrates.

Take daily walks.

Practice high-intensity interval training.

Monitor your calorie intake.

Use olive oil.

Eat balanced and varied meals.

Cut out sodas and sugary drinks.

Eat slowly.

Do intermittent fasting.

Cut out alcoholic beverages.

Adopt low-calorie foods.

Practice yoga or meditation.

Use the stairs instead of the elevator.

Always prefer homemade meals.

Control stress and anxiety.

Do flexibility exercises.

Use food control apps.

Eat healthy fats, like avocado.

Avoid sandwiches.

Use smaller plates.

Replace snacks with fresh fruit.

Practice good humor

Have determination.

Practice swimming.

Use bicycle as transport.

Choose whole foods.

Eat weekly pre-planned meals.

Do Pilates exercises.

Jump rope.

Reduce salt consumption.

Avoid fast food.

Stretch daily.

Choose roasts.

Dance as exercise.

Try circuit training.

Think before you eat.

Cook with coconut oil.

Clean the house with energy.

Consume yogurt daily.

Read food labels.

Eat slowly and savor.

Avoid eating before bed.

Exercise outdoors.

Colorful and varied meals.

Use natural seasonings.

Play team sports.

Replace sweets with fruit.

Use body oils.

Wake up early.

Eat rich in fiber foods.

No refined sugar.

Use Salads.

Do physical activities with friends.

Re-educate yourself to reduce stress.

Avoid excess caffeine.

Listen to music.

Get localized massage.

Replace fats with vegetables in the preparation.

Keep a food diary.

Practice rock climbing for exercise.

Do exercises with a Swiss Ball.

Eat oats for breakfast.

Don't think about food.

Low-calorie meals.

Avoid dairy products.

Consume dried fruits.

Practice water sports.

Reduce your salt intake.

Eat fish regularly.

Do workouts with elastic bands.

Avoid consuming processed foods.

Take aerobic boxing classes.

Use apple cider vinegar occasionally.

Eat nuts and seeds.

Opt for lean meats.

Eat gluten-free meals.

Practice weight training regularly.

Don't eat while watching TV.

Less red meat.

Outdoor activities.

Pepper in food.

Exercise with TRX.

Teas are allies.

Do CrossFit workouts.

Use oregano.

Lemon daily.

Green tea replacing soft drinks.

Take kickboxing classes.

Vegetables for Dinner.

Take Zumba classes.

Replace bread with whole grain options.

Cut carbs at dinner.

Balance exercises.

Use flaxseed oil.

Have a fitness plan.

anarubia.cartas@gmail.com

PERSONALIZED STUDY

wz+34698351431

Made in the USA
Monee, IL
07 November 2024

69602228R00046